SUPER EASY GUITAR
MUSIC FOR BEGIN

BY KIRK TATNALL & SCOTT CU

ISBN: 9798386345341

HOW TO GET THE AUDIO

The free audio files for this book are available to download or stream at: *troynelsonmusic.com*.

We are available to help you with your audio downloads and any other questions you may have. Simply email *help@troynelsonmusic.com*.

See below for the recommended ways to listen to the audio:

Download Audio Files

- Download Audio Files (Zipped)

- Recommended for COMPUTERS on WiFi

- A ZIP file will automatically download to the default "downloads" folder on your computer

- Recommended: download to a desktop/laptop computer *first*, then transfer to a tablet or cell phone

- Phones & tablets may need an "unzipping" app such as iZip, Unrar, or Winzip

- Download on WiFi for faster download speeds

Stream Audio Files

- Recommended for CELL PHONES & TABLETS

- Bookmark this page

- Simply tap the PLAY button on the track you want to listen to

- Files also available for streaming or download at: *soundcloud.com/troynelsonbooks*

To download the companion audio files for this book, **visit:** troynelsonmusic.com/audio-downloads/

INTRODUCTION

Welcome to *Super Easy Guitar Sheet Music for Beginners*! This timeless collection of music is designed to help beginning guitarists of all ages learn songs quickly and easily. Playing the guitar is extremely enjoyable, and one of my goals as an author, musician, and educator is to offer arrangements that are accessible to those who are interested in learning more about the guitar and music in general. I want everyone to find enjoyment in playing the guitar, no matter their skill level.

What differentiates this book from other guitar songbooks? Glad you asked. The most notable differences are:

- **Music Size:** The staffs and notes are enlarged so the music is easier to read.

- **Note Names:** The names of the notes are clearly displayed inside extra-large noteheads.

- **Guitar Tab:** Tab notation ensures that you'll find the correct note. Each line represents a string. The bottom line is your thickest string (low E, string 6) and the top line is your thinest string (high E, string 1). A number placed on a line indicates the fret and string on which the note is played, respectively. For example, a "3" on the top (highest) line indicates that you play fret 3, string 1, and a "0" on the lowest line means play string 6 open (no fingers).

- **Chord Frames:** The chords for each song are provided above the staff. If you'd like to add them to the arrangement, simply use the chord frames and strum along.

- **Melody and Harmony Together:** If you're playing the melody solo, you'll sound fuller if you use the simple two-note chords in the arrangements. To further simplify the melodies, however, you can omit the lower note of each two-note chord and play just the highest (top) note.

- **Key Signatures:** Key signatures are included but accidentals (sharps, flats, and naturals) have been provided in the arrangements for ease of use. Some pieces have been arranged in keys that are different from the original compositions to make them easier to play.

- **Audio Tracks:** Listen to the corresponding audio tracks to get a feel for the songs before you play them.

THE BASICS

THE MUSIC ALPHABET

The letters of the music alphabet are:

A B C D E F G

These letters are assigned to notes on a staff consisting of five lines and four spaces. The notes that appear on the lines are:

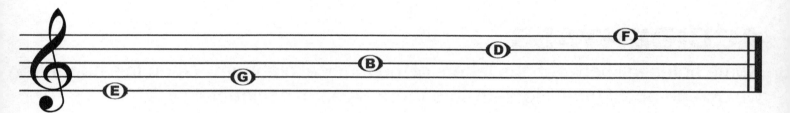

An easy way to memorize these five notes is to use a phrase in which each word begins with the letter on the staff:

Every **G**ood **B**oy **D**oes **F**ine

The notes that appear in the four spaces are:

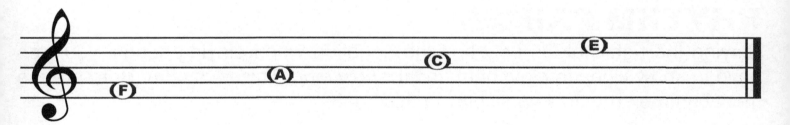

You may have noticed that these four notes, from bottom to top, spell the word **F A C E**, which makes them easy to remember.

Notes that appear *above* or *below* the staff require a *ledger line*, which is a short line that extends the range of the staff.

TIME SIGNATURE

The *time signature* consists of two numbers. For the purpose of this book, we'll focus on the top number, which indicates how many beats are in a *measure*, the space between the vertical lines along the staff.

Three Beats

3
4

Four Beats

4
4

ACCIDENTALS

Some notes fall between the letters of the musical alphabet. When this happens, we use an *accidental*. Here are the three types of accidentals:

Sharp Sign

♯

Flat Sign

♭

Natural Sign

♮

A sharp sign *raises* the pitch of a note by a half step. A flat sign *lowers* the pitch by a half step. A natural sign cancels the sharp or flat.

RHYTHM PRIMER

Playing the right note is only half the equation when playing songs; you also have to know *when* to play them and for *how long*. This is rhythm. Here are the most common rhythms you'll play in this book:

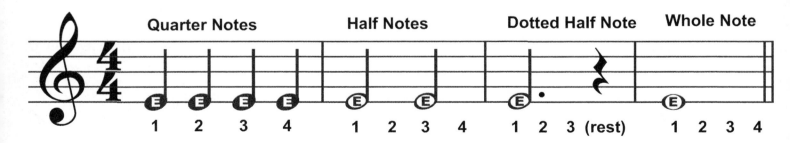

PATRIOTIC & FOLK SONGS

AMERICA
(MY COUNTRY 'TIS OF THEE)

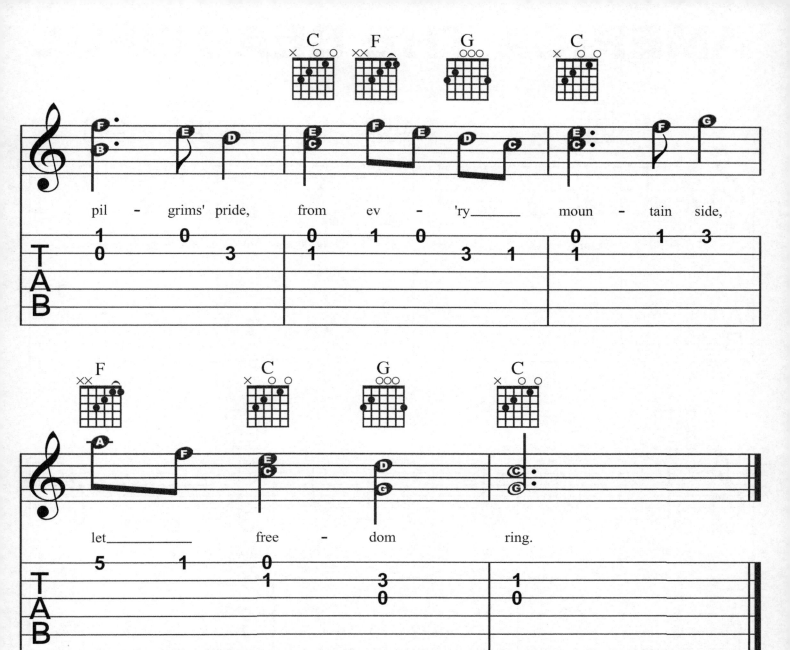

pil - grims' pride,   from   ev -   'ry_____   moun - tain side,

let_____   free -   dom   ring.

AMERICA THE BEAUTIFUL

mer - i - ca, God shed His grace on thee, and

crown thy good with broth - er - hood from

sea to shin - ing sea.

11

CAMPTOWN RACES

13

HOME ON THE RANGE

Oh, give me a home where the buf - fa - lo roam, and the deer and the an - te - lope play. _____ Where sel - dom is heard a dis - cour - ag - ing word, and the

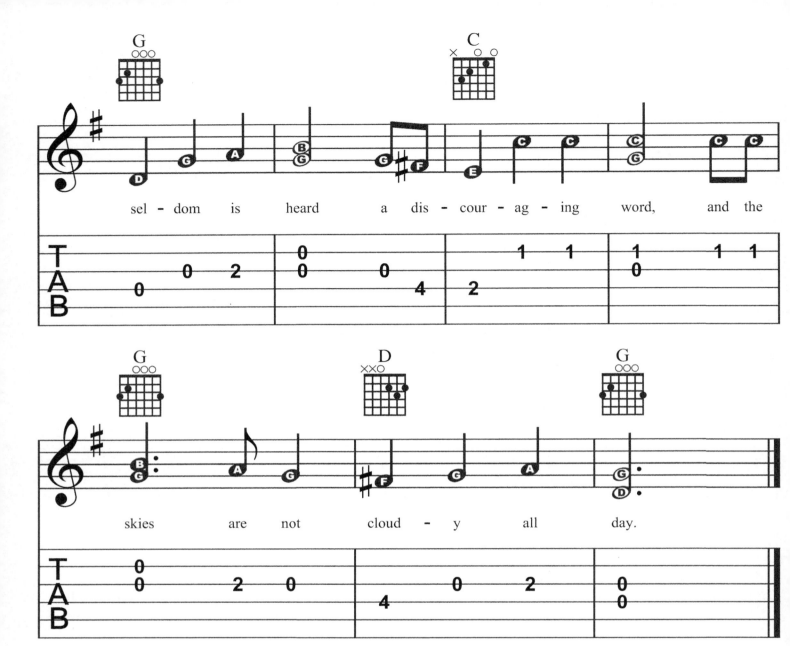

sel - dom   is   heard   a   dis - cour - ag - ing   word,   and the

skies   are   not   cloud - y   all   day.

16

OH MY DARLING, CLEMENTINE

19

OH! SUSANNA

don't you cry for me! For I come from Al – a–

bam – a with a ban – jo on my knee.

ON TOP OF OLD SMOKY

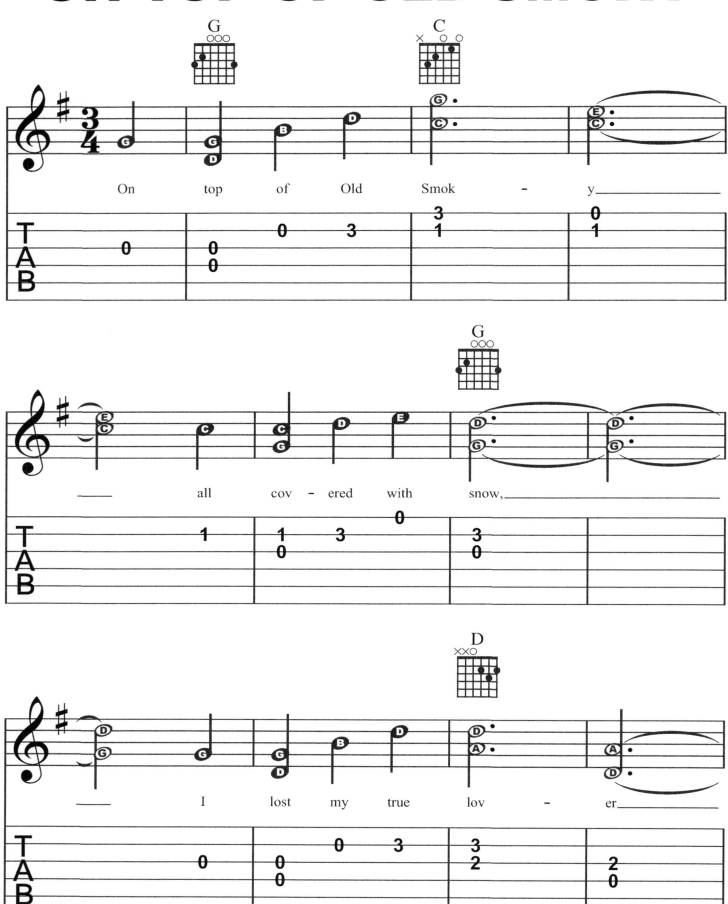

On top of Old Smok - y____ all cov - ered with snow,____ I lost my true lov - er____

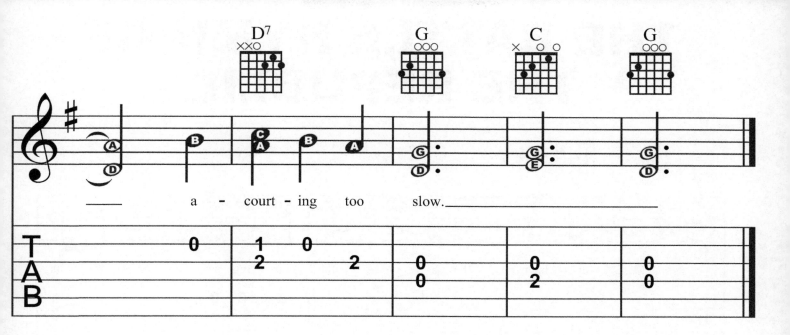

a - court - ing too slow.

THE BATTLE HYMN OF THE REPUBLIC

THE YELLOW ROSE OF TEXAS

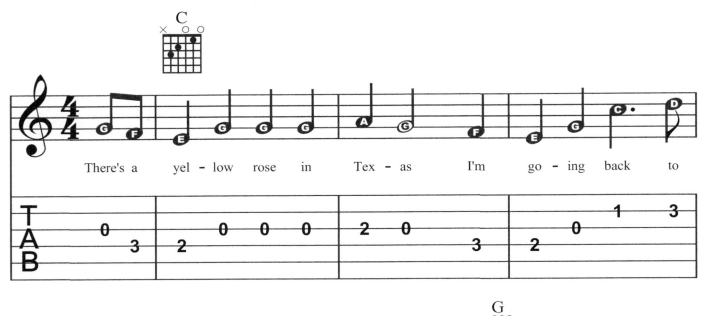

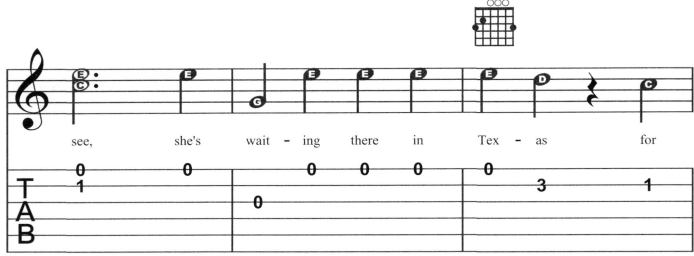

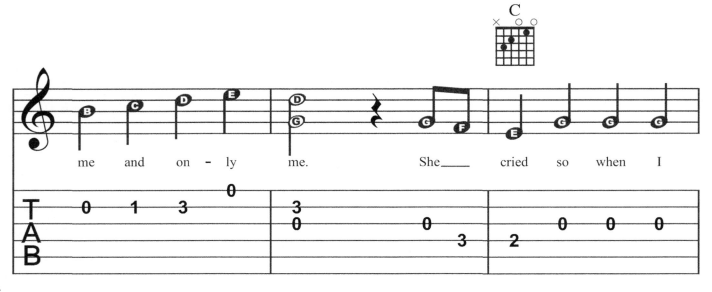

YANKEE DOODLE

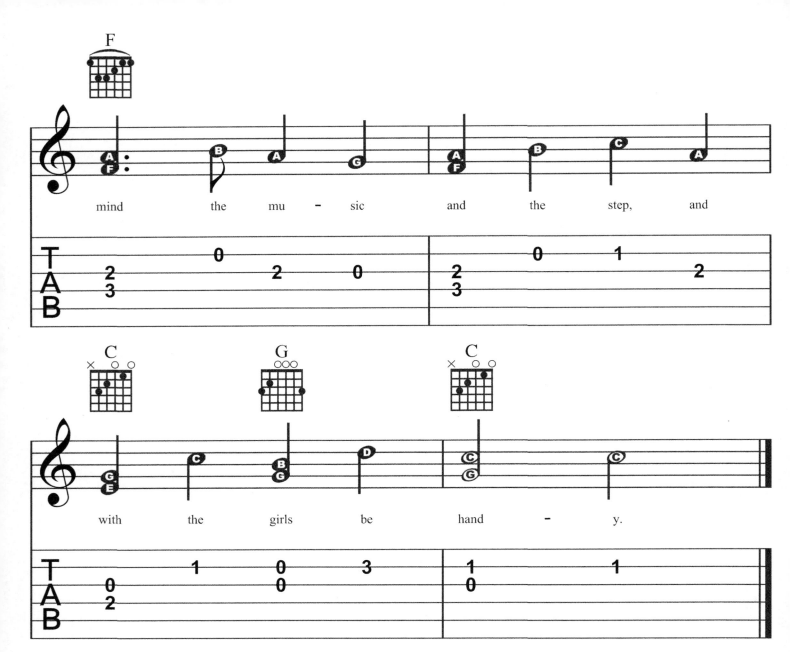

NURSERY RHYMES

ARE YOU SLEEPING?

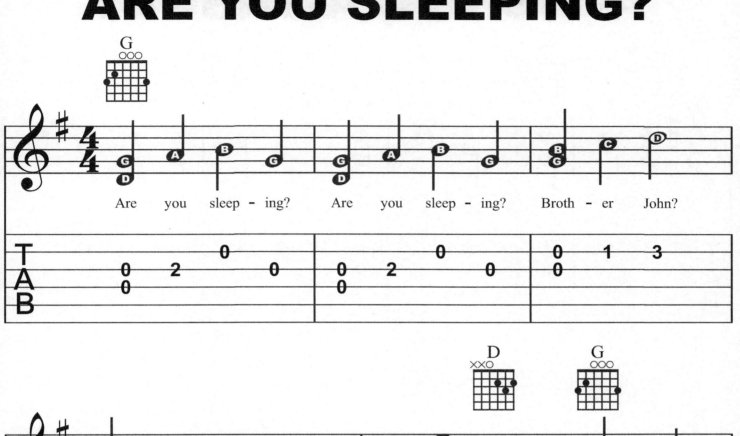

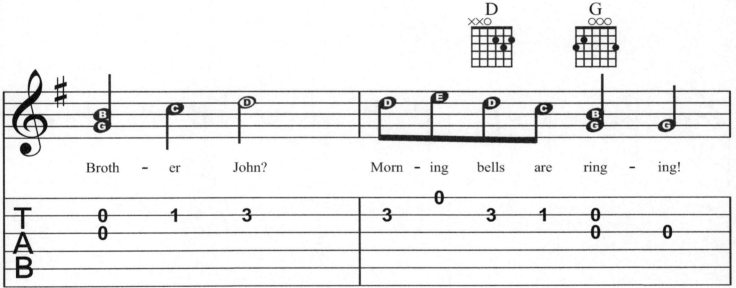

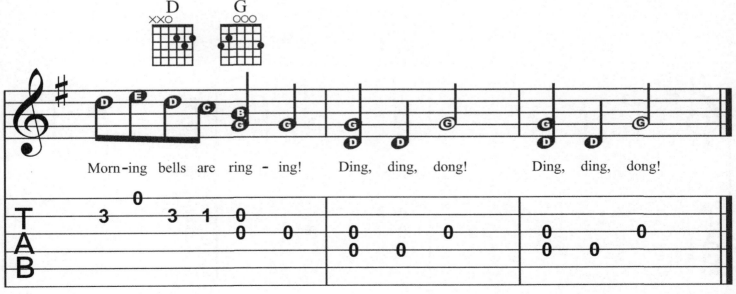

A-TISKET, A-TASKET

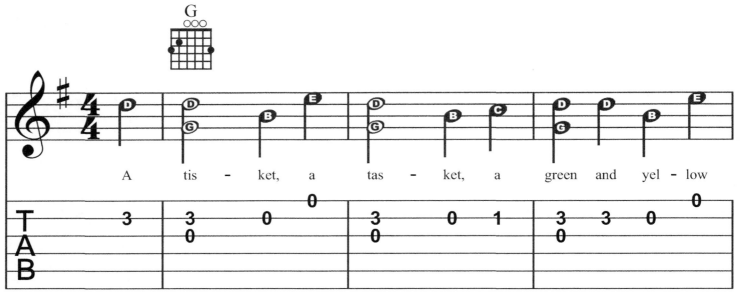

A tis - ket, a tas - ket, a green and yel - low

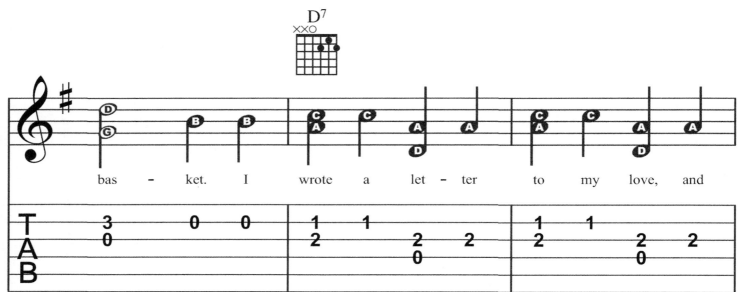

bas - ket. I wrote a let - ter to my love, and

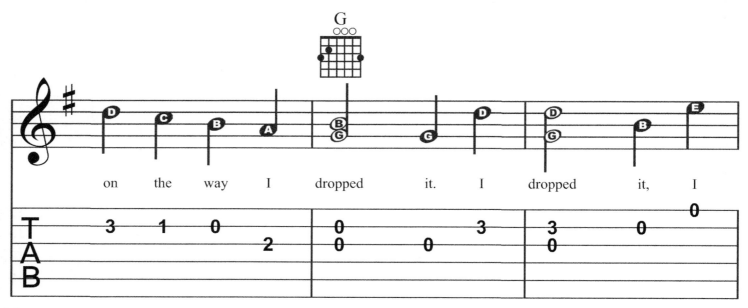

on the way I dropped it. I dropped it, I

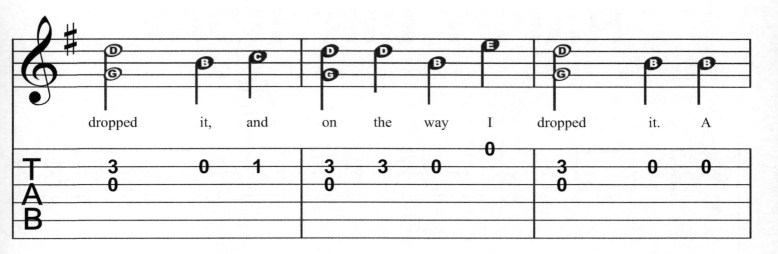

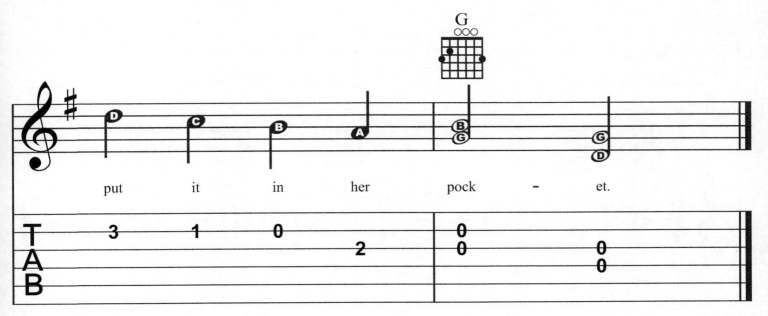

HAPPY BIRTHDAY

LONDON BRIDGE IS FALLING DOWN

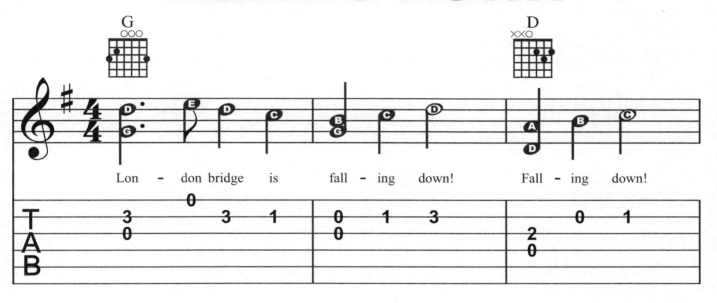

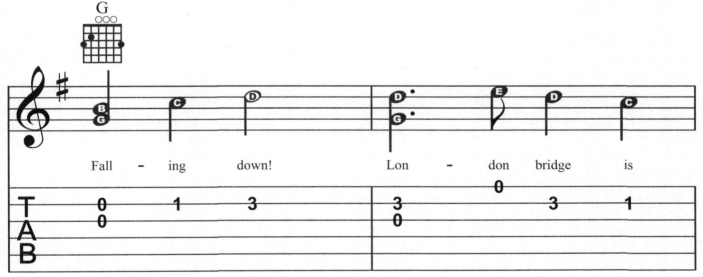

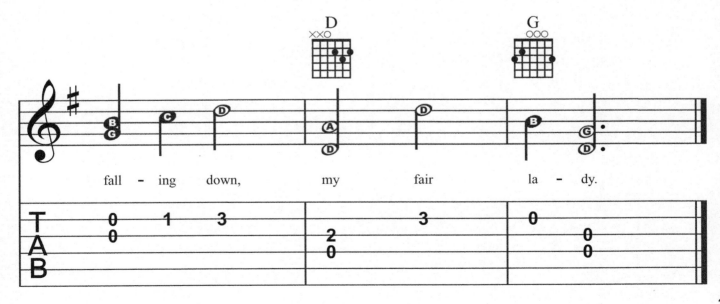

MARY HAD A LITTLE LAMB

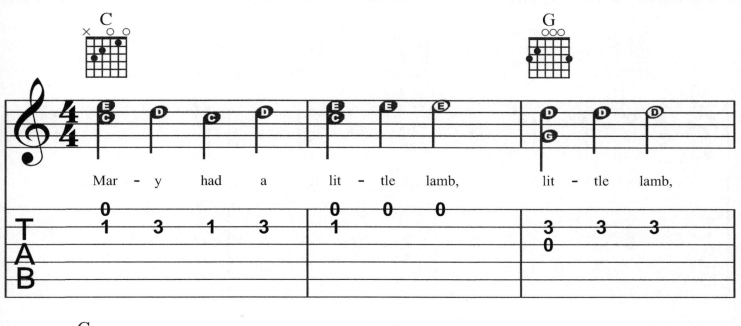

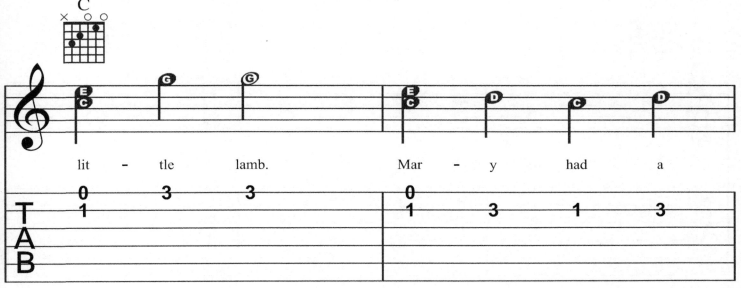

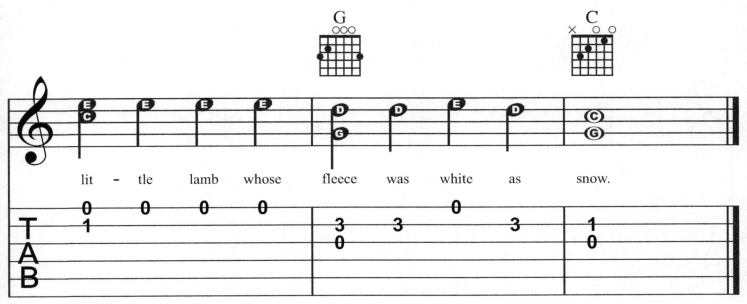

OLD MACDONALD

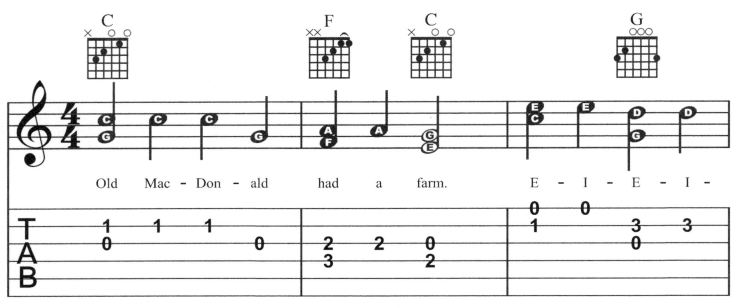

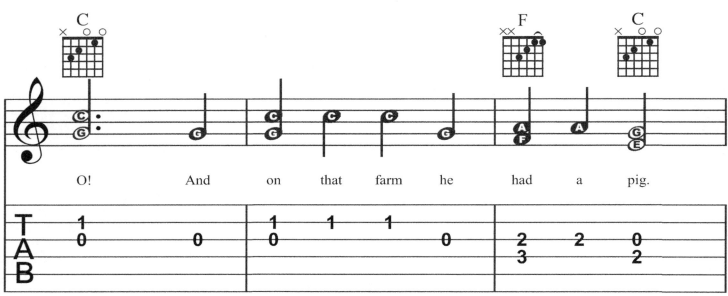

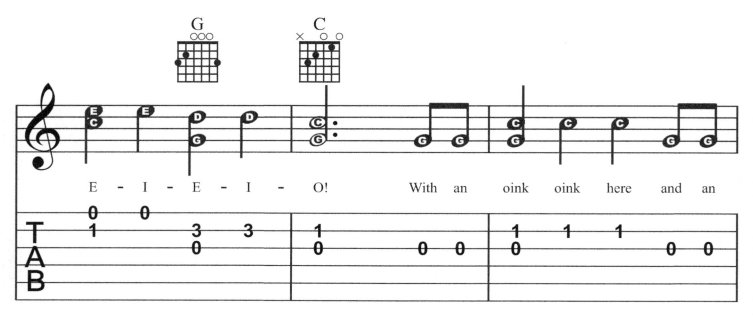

oink   oink   there!   Here an oink, there an oink.   Ev'-ry where an oink   oink!

Old   Mac – Don – ald   had   a   farm.

F   C

G   C

E – I – E – I – O!

THE MUFFIN MAN

THIS OLD MAN

THREE BLIND MICE

carv - ing knife. Did you   ev - er   see such   a

sight   in   your life,   as   three   blind   mice?

TWINKLE, TWINKLE LITTLE STAR

CHRISTMAS CAROLS

AWAY IN A MANGER

DECK THE HALLS

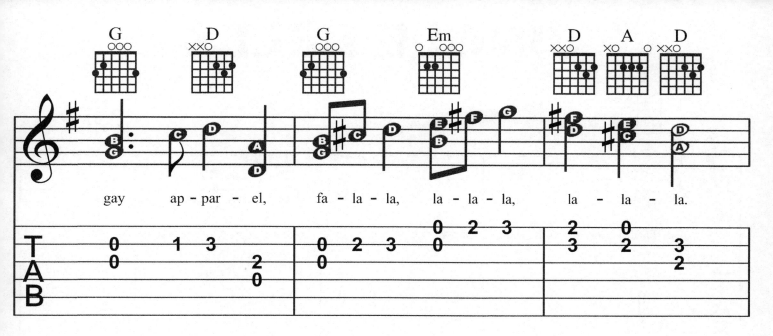

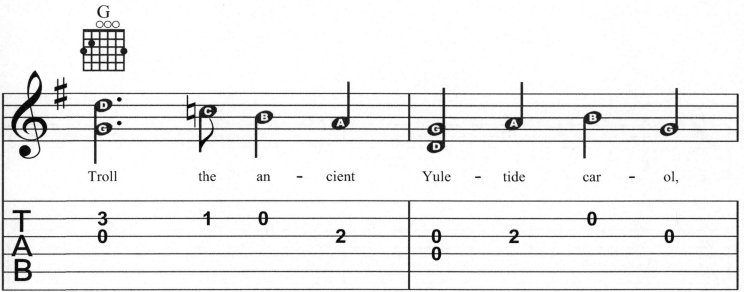

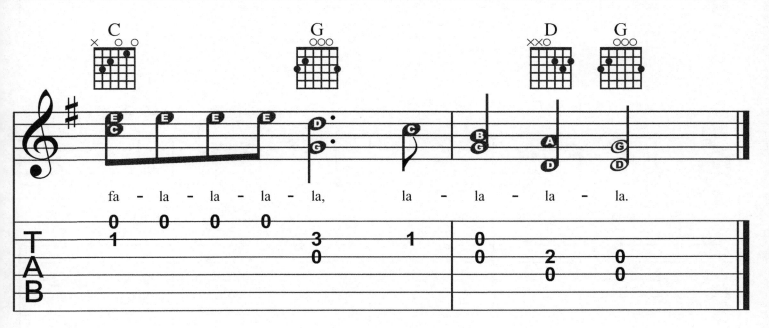

JINGLE BELLS

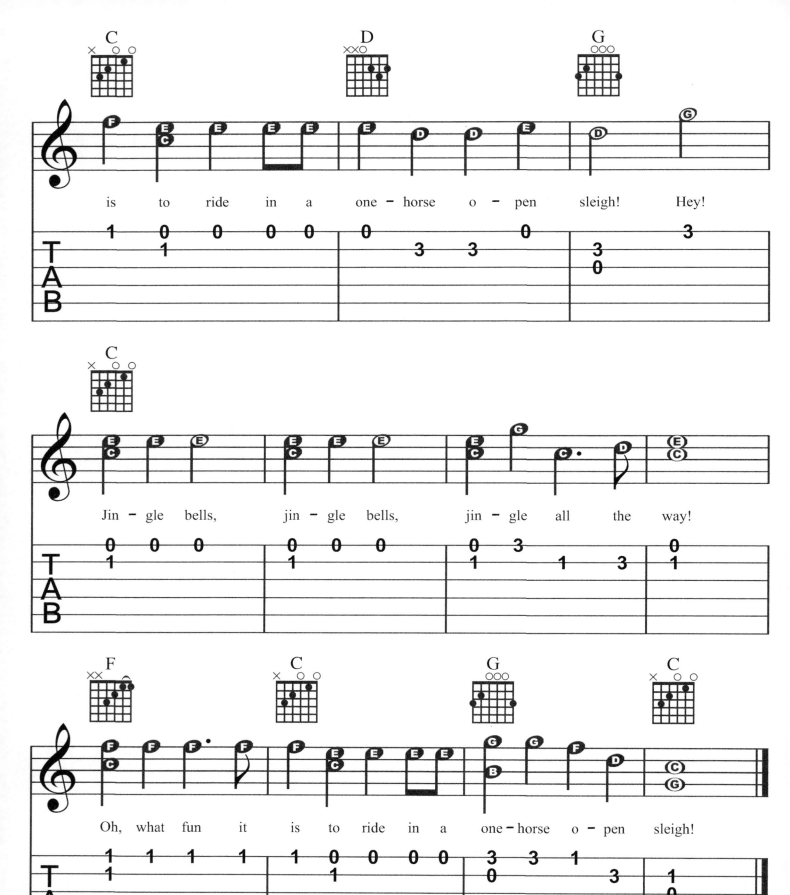

JOY TO THE WORLD

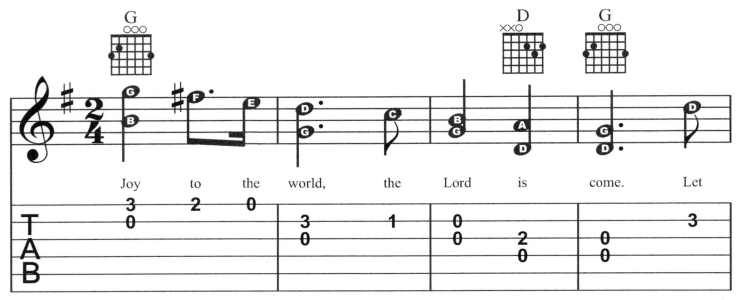

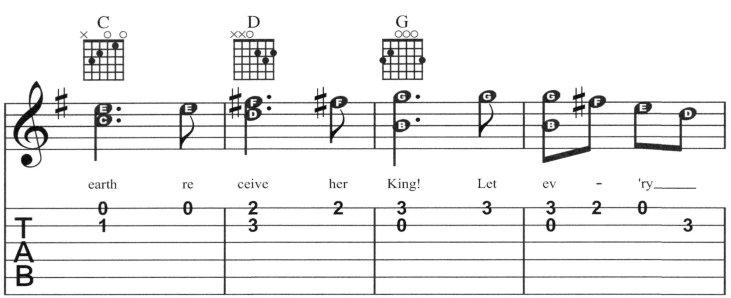

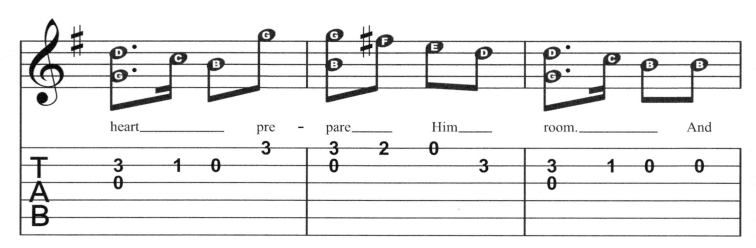

Heav'n and na - ture___ sing! And___ Heav'n and na - ture___ sing! And___

Heav'n,___ and Heav'n_____ and na - ture sing!

O CHRISTMAS TREE

O COME, ALL YE FAITHFUL

O come, all ye faith - ful, joy - ful and tri -
um - phant! O come ye, O come___ ye to
Beth - le hem. Come and be - hold Him,

O COME, O COME EMMANUEL

SILENT NIGHT

UP ON THE HOUSETOP

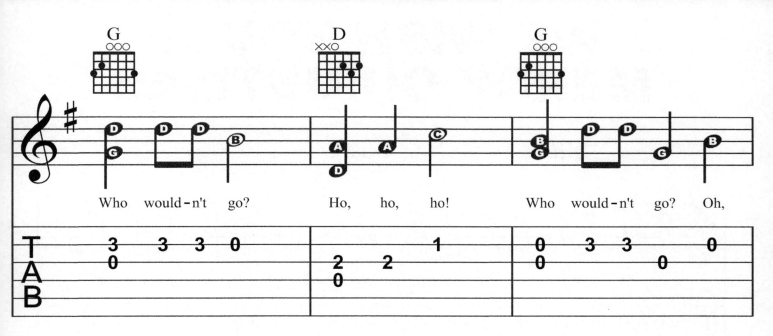

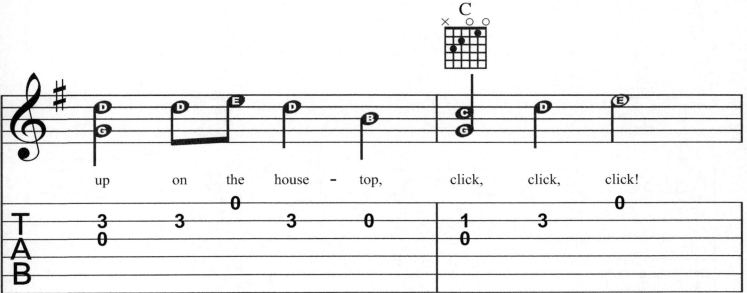

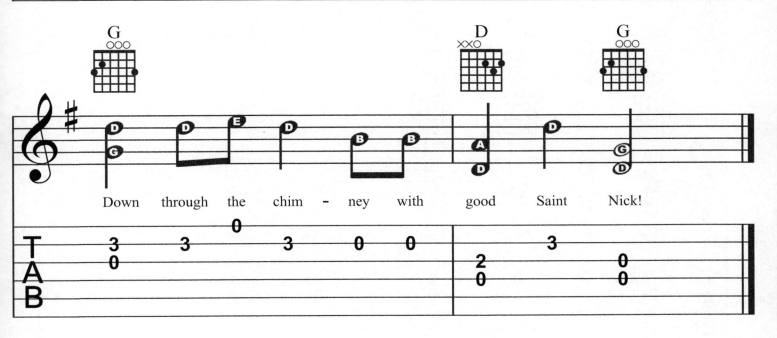

WE WISH YOU A MERRY CHRISTMAS

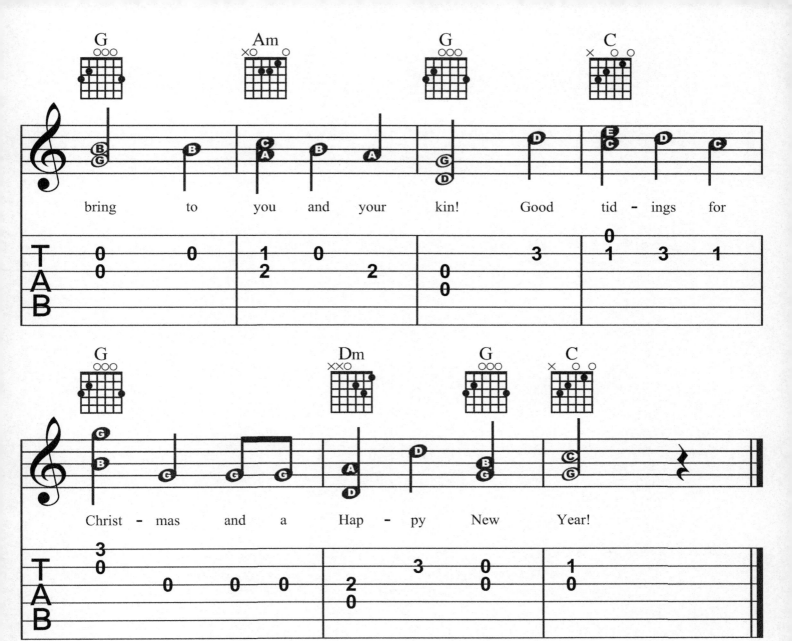

CLASSICAL THEMES

BRAHMS LULLABY

EINE KLEINE NACHTMUSIK

FÜR ELISE

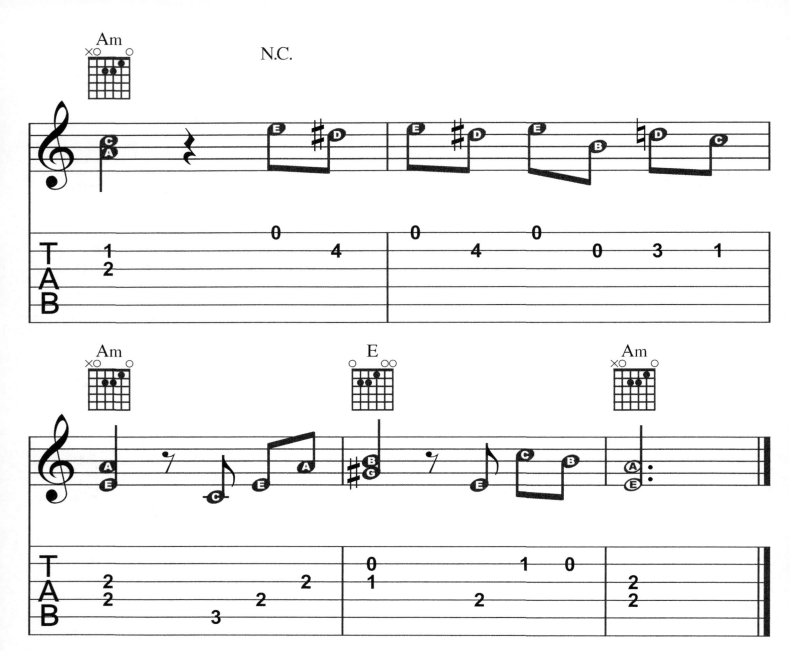

JESU, JOY OF MAN'S DESIRING

MINUET IN G

ODE TO JOY

RONDO ALLA TURCA

THE BLUE DANUBE

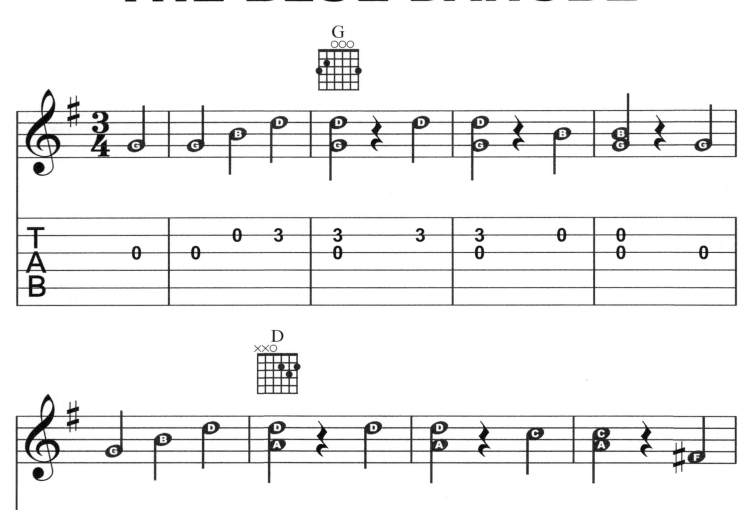

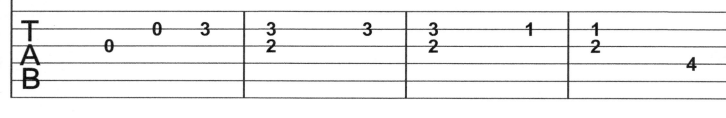

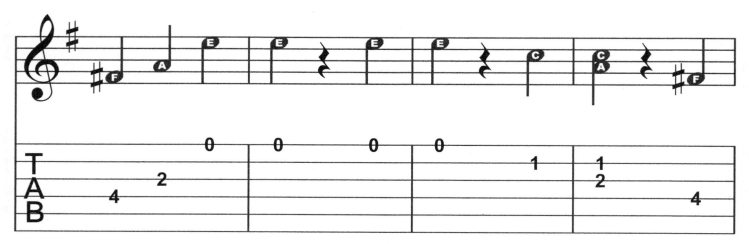

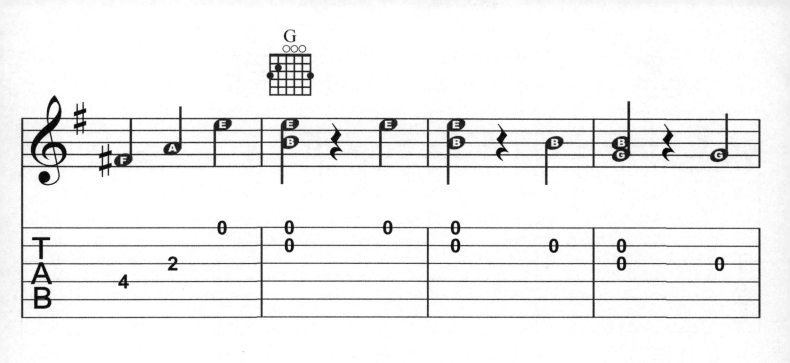

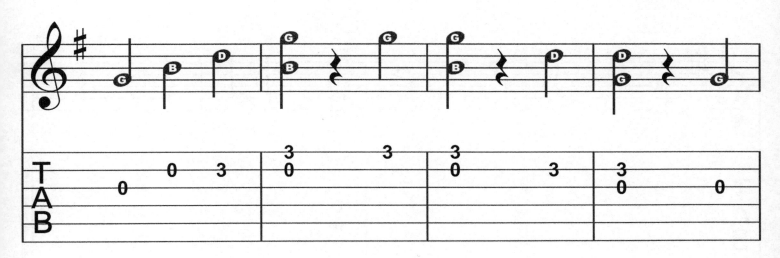

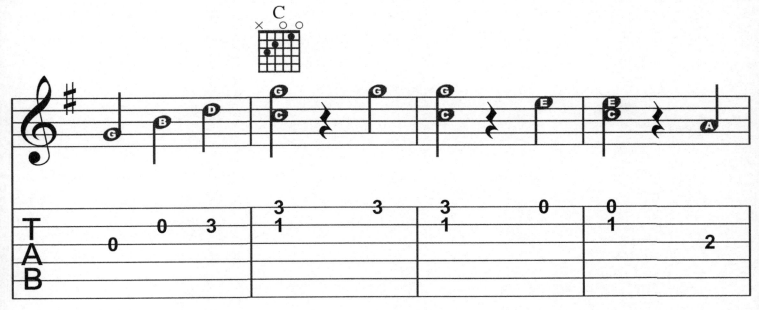

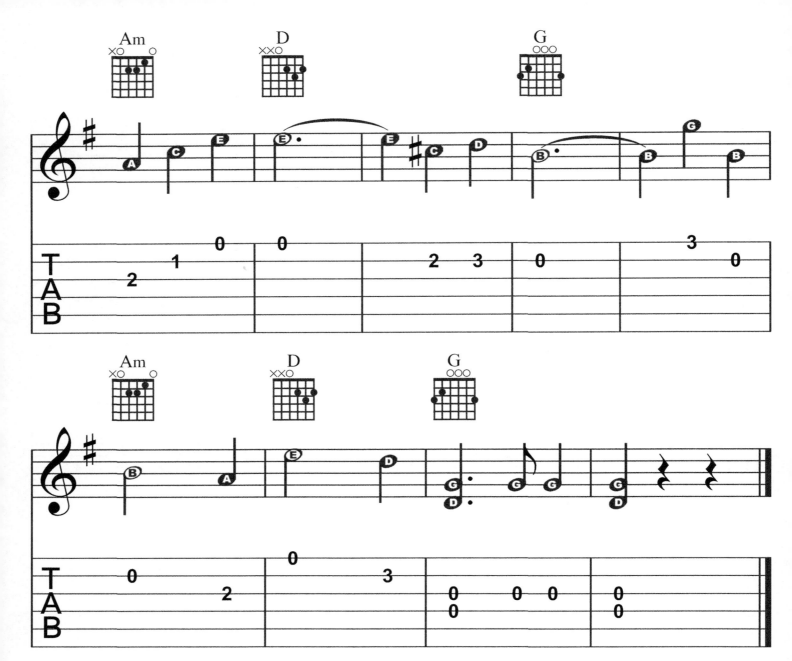

THE ENTERTAINER

WILLIAM TELL OVERTURE

HYMNS &
GOSPELS

AMAZING GRACE

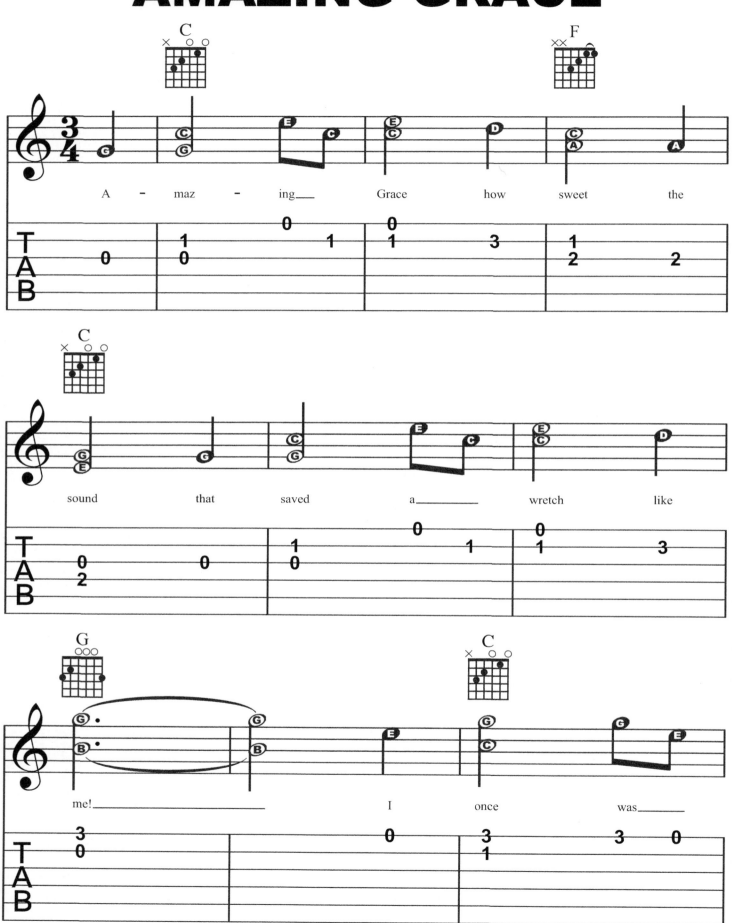

BLESSED ASSURANCE

COME, THOU FOUNT OF EVERY BLESSING

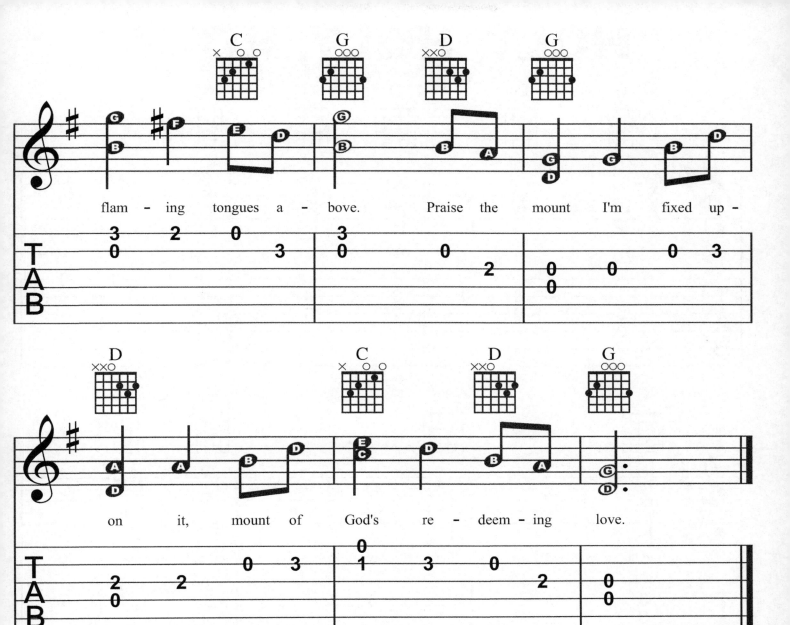

flam - ing tongues a - bove. Praise the mount I'm fixed up -

on it, mount of God's re - deem - ing love.

HOLY, HOLY, HOLY

I SURRENDER ALL

All to Je - sus I sur - ren - der, all to Him I

free - ly give. I will ev - er love and trust Him,

in His pres - ence dai - ly live. I sur - ren - der

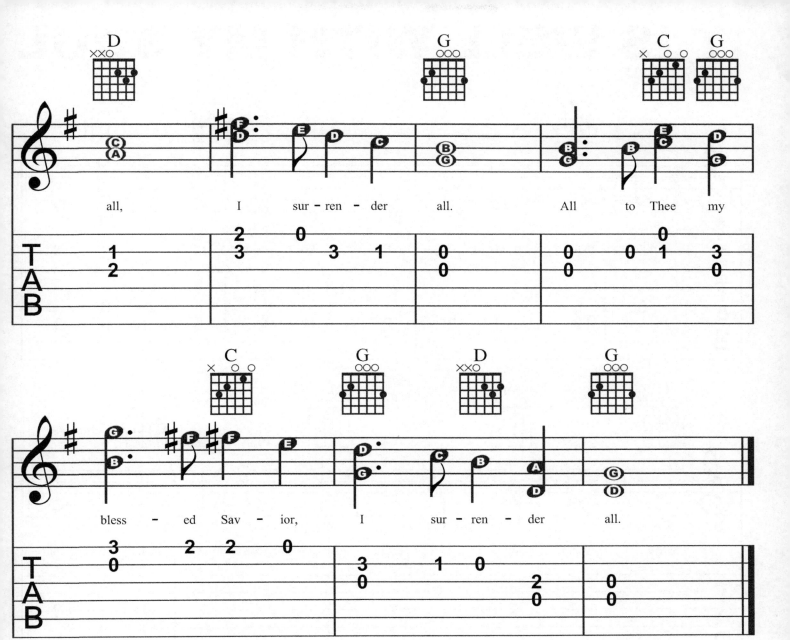

IT IS WELL WITH MY SOUL

JESUS LOVES ME

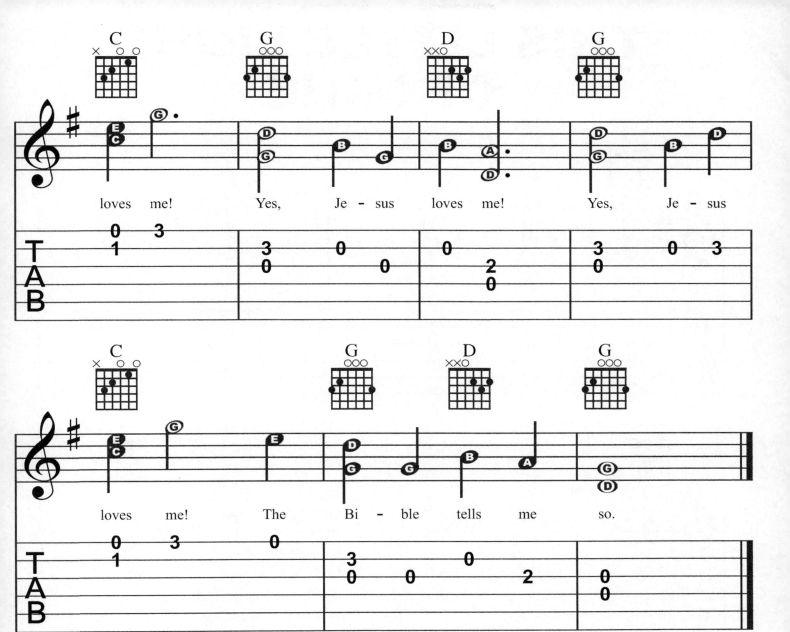

THIS LITTLE LIGHT OF MINE

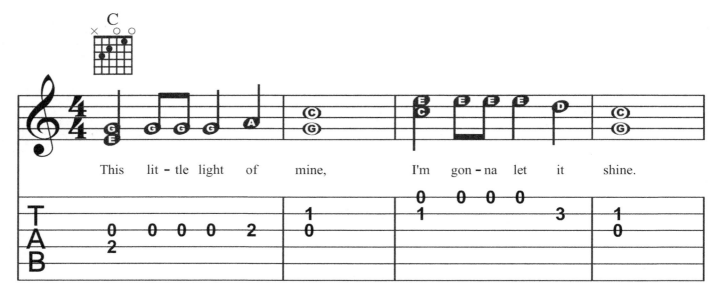

This lit – tle light of mine, I'm gon – na let it shine.

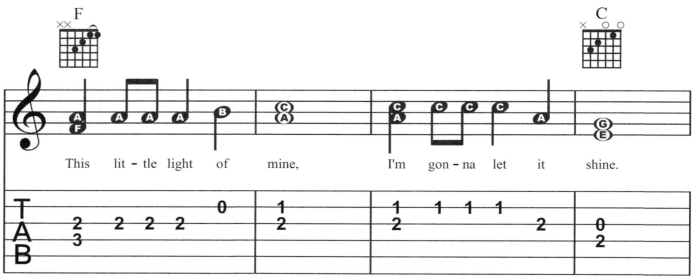

This lit – tle light of mine, I'm gon – na let it shine.

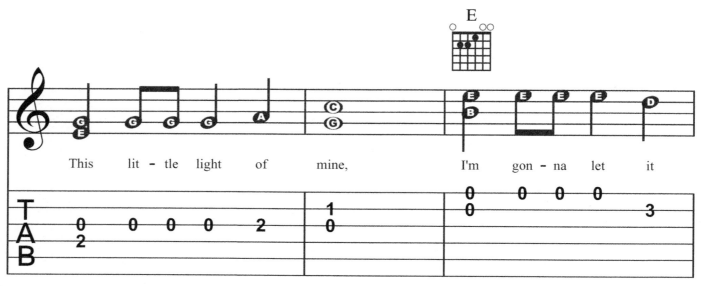

This lit – tle light of mine, I'm gon – na let it

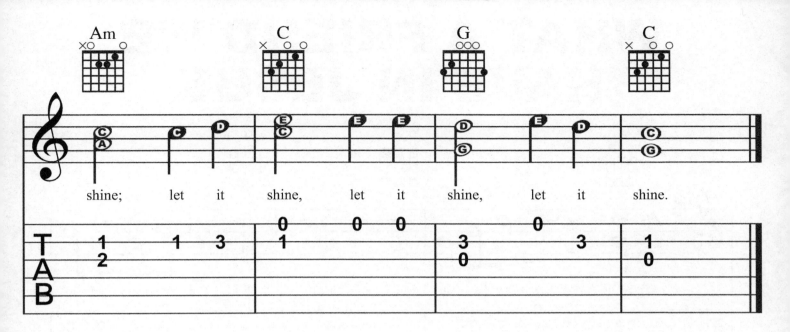

shine;   let   it   shine,   let   it   shine,   let   it   shine.

WHAT A FRIEND WE HAVE IN JESUS

WHEN THE SAINTS GO MARCHING IN

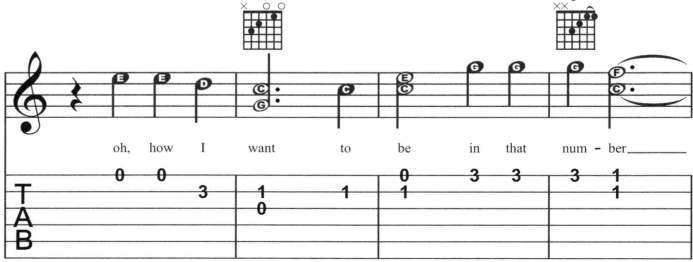

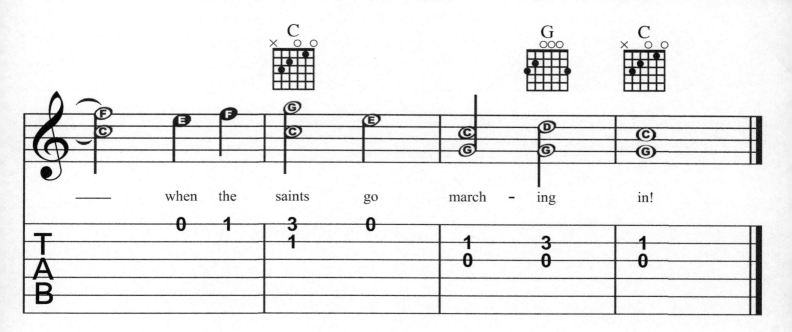

—— when the saints go march – ing in!

Printed in Great Britain
by Amazon

44394043R00066